Fact Finders

LAND and WATER

Lake Ontario

by Anne Ylvisaker

Consultant:
Rosanne W. Fortner, Professor of Natural R
and Associate Director, F. T. Stone Labo
The Ohio State University
School of Natural Resources
Columbus, Ohio

D1299587

Capstone
press

Mankato, Minnesota

Fact Finders is published by Capstone Press,
151 Good Counsel Drive, P.O. Box 669, Mankato, Minnesota 56002.
www.capstonepress.com

Library of Congress Cataloging-in-Publication Data
Ylvisaker, Anne.
    Lake Ontario / by Anne Ylvisaker.
    p. cm.—(Fact finders. Land and water)
    Summary: Discusses Ontario, the smallest of the five Great Lakes, its creation, history, people, industry, and present uses.
    Includes bibliographical references and index.
    ISBN 0-7368-2211-9 (hardcover)
    ISBN 0-7368-6167-X (softcover)
    1. Ontario, Lake (N.Y. and Ont.)—Juvenile literature. [1. Ontario, Lake (N.Y. and Ont.)]
I. Title. II. Series.
F556.Y58 2004
974.7'9—dc21   2003001130

Editorial Credits

Erika L. Shores, editor; Juliette Peters, series designer and illustrator; Alta Schaffer,
    photo researcher; Eric Kudalis, product planning editor

Photo Credits

Cover image: Sailboats on Lake Ontario near Fort Niagara State Park, James P. Rowan

AP Photo/Don Heupel, 21
George Skadding/Timepix, 23
Hamilton, Ontario Tourism, 24–25
Houserstock/Dave G. Houser, 15, 19, 26; Jan Butchofsky, 1, 11, 27
National Archives of Canada, 4–5
Rochester Images: Rochester Public Library Local History Collection, 16–17
Stock Montage Inc., 12–13, 14
Visuals Unlimited/Rob & Ann Simpson, 10

The Hands On activity on page 29 was adapted with permission from *Paddle-to-the-Sea* by M. Seager, R. W. Fortner, and T. Taylor, Columbus, Ohio: Ohio Sea Grant Publications, 1991.

1 2 3 4 5 6 08 07 06 05 04 03

Table of Contents

Chapter 1

Lake Ontario

On May 5, 1814, British commander Sir James Yeo prepared for battle. The next day, he and 500 soldiers would attack American troops at Fort Oswego on Lake Ontario.

The British were fighting the United States in the War of 1812 (1812–1815). Both sides wanted control of the Great Lakes and its nearby areas.

On May 6, the British ships *Montreal* and *Niagara* began firing rockets and guns at Fort Oswego. Other British ships soon landed on the shores near the fort. British officers led the troops toward the fort. British Lieutenant John Hewett ran up a steep hill toward the fort's flagpole.

On May 6, 1814, the British attacked American troops at Fort Oswego on Lake Ontario.

American soldiers shot at Hewett as he climbed the pole and tore down the American flag.

Soon, the British defeated the American troops. The British set the fort on fire after gathering 1,000 barrels of salt, flour, and pork that had been stored there.

The Great Lakes

The Great Lakes of North America are Lake Superior, Lake Huron, Lake Michigan, Lake Erie, and Lake Ontario. Rivers, straits, and canals connect the Great Lakes to each other and to the ocean. Together, the rivers, canals, and lakes make up the St. Lawrence Seaway. The seaway is an important shipping route from the Atlantic Ocean to ports on the Great Lakes.

Like most Great Lakes, Lake Ontario lies between the United States and Canada. The Canadian province of Ontario and the U.S. state of New York border Lake Ontario.

Lake Ontario is the smallest of the Great Lakes. It is 193 miles (311 kilometers) long and 53 miles (85 kilometers) wide. Lake Ontario

Lake Ontario is the smallest Great Lake.

is the second deepest of the Great Lakes.
The average depth is 283 feet
(86 meters). Some areas of the lake
are as deep as 802 feet (244 meters).

Chapter 2

Lake Beginnings

Thousands of years ago, huge sheets of ice covered the Great Lakes area. These glaciers were more than 1 mile (1.6 kilometers) thick. Glaciers pressed down the land. Glaciers also moved rocks that scraped the earth. Together, the pressure and scraping carved wide valleys. Over time, the glaciers melted. The Great Lakes were made when water filled the valleys.

Over thousands of years, Lake Ontario has changed. Today, Lake Ontario has both rocky and sandy shores. Wetlands surround Lake Ontario. The wetlands are home to many kinds of birds and plants.

CANADA

ONTARIO

N
W · E
S

Sackets
Harbor •

Oshawa •

Toronto
★

Lake Ontario

• Rochester

• **Hamilton**

Niagara
Falls

Niagara
River

Welland Canal

NEW YORK

Lake Erie

UNITED STATES

LEGEND	
- - -	Canal
★	Capital
•	City
▭	Lake
◯	Niagara Falls

9

Niagara Falls forms a border between the United States and Canada.

Niagara Falls and the Welland Canal

Rushing water from the Niagara River falls over high cliffs to form Niagara Falls. Over the years, the rushing water has worn away the cliffs. Due to the constant wear, the falls are now 7 miles (11 kilometers) behind their original spot. Erosion moves the falls up the Niagara River about 3 feet (1 meter) every year.

Niagara Falls made it difficult for ships to travel through the Great Lakes. The Niagara River joins Lakes Erie and Ontario. Ships could not travel between them because of the falls. In 1829, the Welland Canal was built. This waterway allows ships to travel around Niagara Falls.

Islands

Lake Ontario flows into the St. Lawrence River. There, the lake washes around 1,500 small islands. The smallest islands are no bigger than cars. The largest island, Wolfe Island, is 49 square miles (127 square kilometers).

Singer Castle sits on Dark Island. This small island is one of the many islands in the St. Lawrence River.

Chapter 3

Early People

Native people lived in the Lake Ontario area when European explorers arrived in the 1600s. The Iroquois Confederacy was the main group of people living there. The Iroquois gave Lake Ontario its name. Ontario means "beautiful lake" or "shining water."

The Great Lakes and the rivers connecting them were important to the Iroquois. The Iroquois fished and traveled on lakes and rivers. They fought other Indian nations for important trading water routes and lands.

Iroquois Indians lived in homes called longhouses.

Explorers and Settlement

French explorer Étienne Brulé came to Lake Ontario in 1615. Huron Indians brought him to the spot that is now Toronto, Ontario.

Later, Frenchman Samuel de Champlain visited the area. He became friends with the Huron. This friendship angered the Iroquois. They did not want the Huron to help the French win control of Lake Ontario.

In the 1760s, the British took control of the Lake Ontario area. British settlers near Lake Ontario stayed loyal to the king of England. After America won the Revolutionary War (1775–1783), British people settled on the Canadian shores of Lake Ontario.

Samuel de Champlain was a French explorer.

They helped Canadians keep their territory during the War of 1812.

Several towns around Lake Ontario began as forts. The forts guarded land and ports during the Revolutionary War and the War of 1812. Later, areas near the forts grew into important industrial and shipping areas.

Fort Henry was built near Lake Ontario during the War of 1812.

Chapter 4

Early Industry

Cities around Lake Ontario became centers for industry in the late 1700s. The capital of Canada's province of Ontario is Toronto. Toronto got its name from the Huron Indian word for "meeting place." French fur traders settled Toronto in 1749. It became a city in 1834. Toronto quickly became Canada's center for industry, trade, and shipping.

Rochester, New York, is another important city near Lake Ontario. Rochester started out as a milling town. Wheat was brought to the mills

Boats called lumber schooners were used to ship lumber from ports on Lake Ontario in the 1800s.

to be turned into flour. People called it "Flour City." The milling industry moved westward in the late 1800s. Rochester then became a mail order center for seeds and shrubs. The city's nickname was changed to "Flower City."

In the 1800s, logging was also an important industry near Lake Ontario. People cut down forests growing around the lake. The trees were turned into lumber for ships, houses, and businesses. Many people moved to cities around the lake to work in sawmills and shipbuilding factories.

Lighthouses

Lighthouses shine bright lights far out into lakes and oceans. The lights help guide ships through dangerous waters or into port. Sailors can also tell where they are by the position of the lights. More than 25 lighthouses guide sailors on Lake Ontario and the St. Lawrence River.

The Prescott Harbor Inner Lighthouse is 40 feet (12 meters) tall.

Chapter 5

Problems

Many years ago, people did not worry about the health of the Great Lakes. Factories dumped waste into the lakes. People often threw trash into the lakes. The polluted water harmed the plants and animals living there.

Water from the other four Great Lakes flows into Lake Ontario. Pollution from the other lakes eventually ends up in Lake Ontario.

Now, the United States and Canadian governments work together to control what goes into the lake. Factories must be careful not to pollute the lake. People work to keep trash out of the lake.

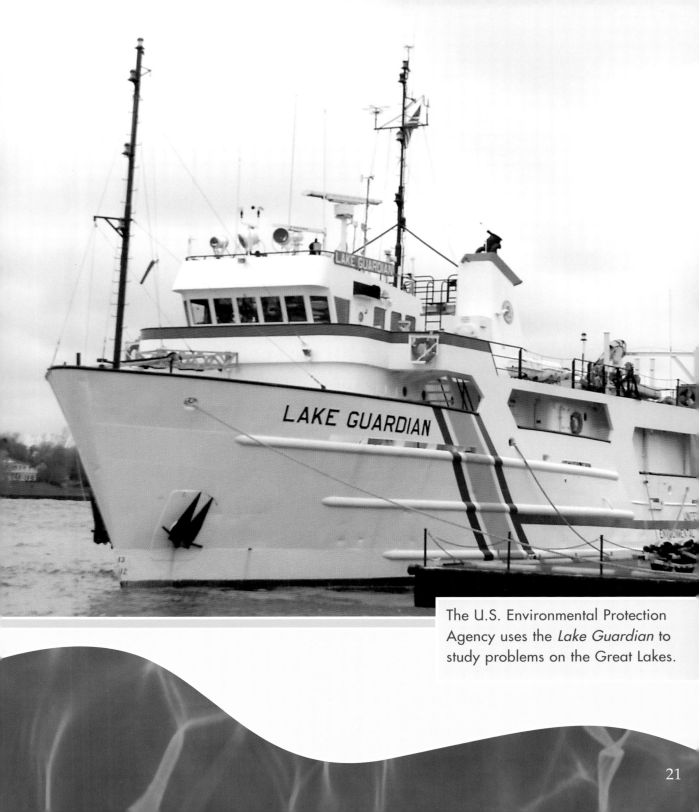

The U.S. Environmental Protection Agency uses the *Lake Guardian* to study problems on the Great Lakes.

Sea Lampreys

Other dangers besides pollution affect Lake Ontario. Fishing is important on Lake Ontario. In 1970, fish in Lake Ontario were harmed by a strange sea creature. Sea lampreys attach to fish. Lampreys suck the blood and other body fluids out of fish.

People began to notice the sea lamprey as fishing became more important on Lake Ontario. Scientists worked to lower sea lamprey populations in Lake Ontario and the other Great Lakes. Scientists blocked streams where lampreys were born. The lampreys could not enter the lakes. Beginning in 1972, people put more fish into Lake Ontario to replace the ones killed by sea lampreys.

Sea lampreys attach themselves to fish.

Chapter 6

Lake Ontario Today

Cities near Lake Ontario are home to important industries. Most of Lake Ontario's industry lies on its Canadian shores. Goods made in Lake Ontario's cities are sent all over the world.

Toronto is an important shipping port. Products shipped here are placed on railroads and airplanes. Toronto also is a center for making books, TV programs, and movies.

Steel is made in Hamilton, Ontario. It is sent to Oshawa, Ontario, and other cities that make cars. Other goods such as tires and farm machinery are also made in Hamilton.

Hamilton, Ontario, is a
large city on Lake Ontario.

Tourism and recreation are also important industries around Lake Ontario. Sailboats dock at Sackets Harbor. Lake Ontario's rocky shores are good for hiking. The sandy beaches are popular tourist spots. Canoeing and kayaking are favorite sports on the lake.

Lake Ontario is important to the people living near it. People want to keep the lake clean. They want to enjoy the lake for years to come.

Lake Ontario's shores are popular places to visit.

People dock their boats at the marinas along Lake Ontario's shores.

Fast Facts ━━━

Length: 193 miles (311 kilometers)

Width: 53 miles (85 kilometers)

Average depth: 283 feet (86 meters)

Maximum depth: 802 feet (244 meters)

Shoreline length: 871 miles (1,402 kilometers)

Population surrounding the lake: 5.6 million

Weather: The area around Lake Ontario has warm summers and cold winters. Heavy rain and snow often occur near Lake Ontario. The lake usually does not freeze in the winter except near the shoreline.

Fish: Many kinds of fish live in Lake Ontario. These fish include Atlantic salmon, lake herring, lake sturgeon, northern pike, walleye, and white bass.

Hands On: Water In and Out

Water flows in and out of the Great Lakes. Rain, snow, and rivers bring water to the lakes. The amount of water entering the other Great Lakes can affect Lake Ontario. Try this activity to see how water levels in the lakes change.

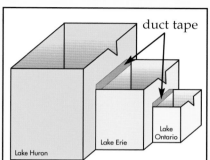

What You Need

Adult helper
Three different-sized milk cartons
Scissors
Duct tape
Ruler   Sink or large dishpan
Black marker   Measuring cup

What You Do

1. Ask an adult to cut the cartons as shown in the diagram above.
2. Use duct tape to attach the cartons as shown in the diagram.
3. Label the biggest carton Lake Huron. Label the middle carton Lake Erie. Label the smallest carton Lake Ontario.
4. Use the ruler to measure 1 inch (2.5 centimeters) below each notch. Draw a line at this spot inside each carton.
5. Place the cartons in a sink or dishpan. Fill each carton with water until you reach the line you marked.
6. Add 1 cup (240 mL) of water to the largest lake. How high above the line is the water now?
7. Add 1 cup (240 mL) of water to the middle lake. How high above the line is the water now? In which lake did the water level change more?
8. Add 1 cup (240 mL) of water to the smallest lake. How high is the water now? Did the water overflow?

How do you think the size of each Great Lake affects its water level? Water entering a large lake can spread out. A lot of water entering a smaller lake might cause it to overflow or flood.

29

Glossary

canal (kun-NAL)—a channel that is dug across land; canals connect bodies of water so that ships can travel between them.

erosion (e-ROH-zhuhn)—the wearing away of something by water or wind

glacier (GLAY-shur)—a large, slow-moving sheet of ice and snow

industry (IN-duh-stree)—businesses that make products or provide services

mill (MIL)—a building that has machines to grind grain into flour or meal

port (PORT)—a place where boats and ships can dock safely

Internet Sites

Do you want to find out more about Lake Ontario? Let FactHound, our fact-finding hound dog, do the research for you.

Here's how:
1) Visit *http://www.facthound.com*
2) Type in the **Book ID** number: **0736822119**
3) Click on **FETCH IT**.

FactHound will fetch Internet sites picked by our editors just for you!

Read More

Beckett, Harry. *Lake Ontario.* Great Lakes of North America. Vero Beach, Fla.: Rourke, 1999.

Rogers, Barbara Radcliffe, and Stillman D. Rogers. *Toronto.* Cities of the World. New York: Children's Press, 2000.

Index